Bonfire of Poetry

EDITORS

Alicia Kimberly

CChristy White

Kenneth Weene

Mark Young

Bonfire of Poetry
Is dedicated to all children who love to read.

The royalties from this book will be donated to THE 12 BOOKS
PROGRAM, an initiative of the Mesa, Arizona, United Way.

The 12 Books Program provides literacy support to help children,
especially those in need to achieve reading proficiency by 4th grade.

Did you know that kids who can't read at grade level by 4th grade
are four times more likely than their peers to drop out of high
school? And, if they live in poverty, they're 13 times more likely.

Dropping out of high school increases a child's chances of
experiencing homelessness, poverty, and incarceration as an adult.
In fact, 2/3 of children who aren't proficient readers by 4th grade
will end up in jail or on welfare.

The 12 Books Program distributes free books to primary grade
students. Owning books and having them available to read helps
mitigate summer learning loss and actually approximates the gains
children achieve by attending summer school.

The 12 Books Program also offers volunteers who spend 30 minutes
twice a week during the school year with children helping them with
their reading and language arts. This is done online and the
participating children are given a free book each week to encourage
their leisure reading outside of school.

We the editors of Bonfire of Poetry are proud to support The 12
Books Program and hope that many of the children who are taking
part in that program will someday join us by writing their own
verse.

Alicia Kimberly; CChristy White; Kenneth Weene; Mark Young

TABLE OF CONTENTS

TINDER   7
        (Section editor Mark Young)

Roswell   Alicia Kimberly   7
I close my eyes   Kenneth Weene   9
Processing Center   Mark States   10
Threading the Warp   John Daleiden   11
Voltaic   Alicia Kimberly   13
Hemingway in Paris   Jack Evans   14
To Touch a Tornado   Alicia Kimberly   16
New Moon Meditation   CChristy White   17
vacation 2022   Mark Young   18

BLAZE   19
        (Section editor CChristy White)

Matthew 24:6   Alicia Kimberly   19
the walls   Artiste   21
Summer to Fall   Carol Tahir   22
The key of wait   Artiste   23
The Storm   Tanya Whitney   24
I want to touch you--   CChristy White   25
Mosquitoes in my village   Umar O. Abdul   26
Heart   Alicia Kimberly   27
Peggy's Blue Skylight   Jack Evans   28
Dinner With My Brother at Zarda BBQ Mark Young   29
To Hide a Child   Cynthia Hogue   31
You the earth, I the plower   Kenneth Weene   33
damp map to a small place   Artiste   34
Flagstaff, She Is on Fire   Susan Vespoli   36
A Dozen (or so) Pieces of Sage Advice
from an Upper-Middle-Aged Man Who…   Mark Young   37
For All the Universe   Alicia Kimberly   39

Good and Bad   Rosemarie Dombrowski 41
Fire Season Again   CChristy White 42

EMBERS   44
(Section editor Kenneth Weene)

Ark   Alicia Kimberly 44
Morning Delivery   Mark Young   47
Paper Sack   Kenneth Weene 48
What Will the Dead Say?   CChristy White 49
I don't care if I never get back   John Daleiden 50
Instead it is dark   Cynthia Hogue 52
Facebook Post   Kenneth Weene 53
The Sadness of Time Passing Jack Evans   54
2 Kings 9:33-37   Alicia Kimberly 55
Poetry Therapy at the Maricopa Reentry
       Center, Week 4   Rosemarie Dombrowski 56
After the War There Was No Food Cynthia Hogue 57
Lullaby   Umar O. Abdul 58
The ghosts were running late last night Kenneth Weene 59
Harmony   Charles Watts   60
Bifröst   Alicia Kimberly 61

ASHES   62
(Section editor Alicia Kimberly)

Take Me Home   Mark Young   62
Five-o'clock   Alicia Kimberly 63
Nous avons le cafard   Kenneth Weene 64
The Pacifist   Cynthia Hogue 66
The Falling Wife   CChristy White 67
A Detuned Piano Reminds Me of
       Her Sadness   Jimmy Broccoli 68
When Her Body Died   Charles Watts   69
Death Watch   Charles Watts   70

If Steve ...   CChristy White   71
listening to Messiaen September, 2020   Kenneth Weene   72
I Wrote My First Poem About You.   Alicia Kimberly 73
Absolution in Limbo   Tanya Whitney   75
Suicide   Adamu Ibrahim Mohammed   76
With Strings Attached   Mark States   77
Poetry Therapy at the Maricopa Reentry
          Center, Week 28   Rosemarie Dombrowski   78
The Paperback   Earnest A. Shoemate   79
Imagine   Mark Young   81
Psalm 23   Alicia Kimberly   82

Contributor Bios   83

TINDER

Alicia Kimberly

Roswell

I've held my eyes wide, incessant, yet never caught
a sasquatch flat glance from the treeline, never felt
phantom mothman wings thunderflap, never known
the divine burn of the Holy Ghost on my tongue–

only the wreck on the highway, the yellow tape
on the door, knifeknuckled vagrants, television
politicians, beadeyed evangelists, electric bills
in the mail, Grandfather in a hospital bed.

If I turn my eyes inside-out, I'm a child, trudging muddy
hills, squashing earthworms between blood-caked toes,
wishing to find monsters, instead watching as the faded
gunmetal of a water tower saucer rises to the south.

The east rolls with ghost story fog, saturated in damp-
haired laughing dead children, crawling, spindle-legged
wendigo, settling imaginary over the corn fields
just a moment before the breeze, filled with drizzlerain

steaming cow's breath tugs it free. It pulls at me
terribly, so I tug up my overalls and run away west
with the wind until I stumble into tree roots, tumble
where my sister sits, pale, knitting doll dresses,

leaves falling around her like torn paper, her cordless radio
static flies low under the tinny thudthud echo of a basketball
on the sidewalk, the tight ding of my brother's bicycle bell.
No matter the length of longing to be afraid of something

unhuman, for a change, the road stretches straight
across hours of New Mexico nothing-brown stillness.

My daughter's green alien-dotted scarf stays warm
around her sleepy neck, uninterrupted midnight tassels

tousling in the hum from the air conditioning vents.
While she dreams of flying saucers, my headlights never waver,
the radio plays steady, the numbers on the clock tell the time.
An owl shakes loose her feathers, a crow lands on the corn.

Kenneth Weene

I close my eyes

       and allow my nostrils to remember
you in the nearly not-quite rain your hair plastered
down around your ears clinging to your dimpled
cheeks as I run my fingers downward towards
your chin tilted ever so slightly up and your lips
waiting for mine waiting for the taste of wine
and figs growing above our heads while we sit
on the patio waiting for the storm of surrender
waiting for new memories and recollections of old-ago
loves in that previous life we must have shared
to have grown so immediately into this one moment
this moment redolent with wine and figs and sweetness
waiting and finding this memory of love

Mark States

Processing Center

These thoughts
first written then balled up and tossed
into a fireplace
whose mantle is adorned
with framed photo of four siblings
red ribbons
and envelopes postmarked a year ago
addressed from "Processing Center"

These thoughts
on second thought not so remarkable
and rather than be reminded
of the need to rethink them
to sit on a couch in between stacks of non-matching pillows
and the remains of last week's bag of potato chips
with pen in hand

it's easier to find the remote control

easier to strike the match till it pops
then drop
and watch tv while log and paper burn
until their aromas
conjure thoughts more suitable to the mood

John Daleiden

Threading the Warp

In the garden
where my son has retreated,
he amuses himself.
There are rugs to weave, books to read—
people come and go . . .
and hours of tedium.
But most of all there is no rain.
No need for umbrellas, no need for overshoes.
His flayed, naked nerves
exposed for all to see,
he plays in the garden.

        Lift the heddle—
        thread the yarn—
        beat the beater—

He says,
"Yesterday, I kissed her lips.
Tomorrow, she will kiss mine."

        Lift the heddle—
        thread the yarn—
        beat the beater—

"My father doesn't love me
and I need his love."

        Lift the heddle—
        thread the yarn—
        beat the beater—

"I don't want to live.
Life is empty."

        Lift the heddle—

> thread the yarn—
> beat the beater—

And there are books to read . . .
word after word . . .
page after page . . .

At least in this garden,
he can sun himself . . .
and if he finds tedium,
it is here he retreats—
it is his choice to come or go.

As for shelter,
his book is umbrella
enough to keep off any rain,
and the carpet he weaves
is a temporary occupation,
a plain view twill or double weave,
a clear design for all to see,
a scented flower, a healing balm.
No need for overshoes
or sheltering umbrellas
in this kind garden.

Alicia Kimberly

Voltaic

to breathe the name of the first woman to wild-eye
an evening electrified aubergine sky, alone, roiling
amaranth ink-blues obstructing any view of the night-
belted lion hunter, her Orion, her cat-pelted Samson,
her armored Heracles.

simultaneous, as possessed of two hearts,
felt both jolt-filled to her brims with swelling storm,
as if she were made of cloud and tempest,
and bereft, unprotected, buffeted by grit and roar
of the violent wind, the wild fanged, prowling felid.

if time were a disc of clay, spun like a record, millenn
ia
would be mere miles of mountain road, winding down
upon itself, crossing back–i stand toe-to-toe with her,
cliffside, breathing in the air she breathes out, fingers
brush as we're held to our moments by centrifuge.

i have the word *gravity*, she does not, yet we both
hold our faces to firmament, willing the weight
of the world to turn inside-out, so our tears would fall
upward to his starry feet–so the universe would stop
expanding, drifting him just out of reach.

Jack Evans

Hemingway in Paris

I

The wind tells him
It is winter
And the rain
The rain is as fragrant
As soft black hair
That falls over bare shoulders
He thinks of Cezanne
And writes of Cezanne
Leaving behind the frailness
And settling on the
Plainness of truth

At the table
Plums and raspberries
Glisten in liquid light
And out of the window
The dampened rooftops
Of Paris stretch out into sunset

II

He reads Georges Simenons long
Into the night
His own work
Fermenting in his pocket
While the silhouette of trees
Like a Giacometti sculpture
Plays against a grey black sky

III

All his first stories had been lost
Like remembrances left

Too long in the
Attic of the mind
Stolen then sold by the letter
In dark alleys to vagrants who
Re-dream them in their sleep

IV

Along the Seine
Barges move against
A diligent wind
Their rigid bows
Like rusty knives
Slice sunrise

On the cusp of new day
When memory is hunger
He sits in a silence
Made of history and fog
Imagining the world as story
And the day ahead
A prelude to moonlight

Alicia Kimberly

To Touch a Tornado

stand on a hill, toes damp in warm mudgrass. watch the storm-swirl
plunge into the sea
-colored marsh. boreas' purple icewings whip stingwind above you,
feel breezes at your feet caress balmly the vivid greens, gentle as a
groom would brush an old, toothless mare. oscillating currents fill
you with fearfreedom, goosebumps crawl up your childlimbs
in the still, heavy pregnancies growing deeper and darker with each
rotation.
sirens build from a low hoovesrumble to a bansheescream
like the second-coming of christ breaking through
the torrents of cold and warm and wet.
your heart breaks electric against the static
negative charge with longing,
the edges of you are pulled
toward the twisting twirlcloud,
fingertips first. you need
to touch it. but you won't.
your mother calls
your name
from the
kitchen window.
you twist
outsidein.
your insides
walk you
back
to
her.

CChristy White

New Moon Meditation

Rituals of release and re-creation
seem to intensify at the new moon,
whose presence is felt rather than seen
and whose shuttered light reveals stars.
In our meditation circle we speak
of who we are, what we intend
as the mountain night blankets us,
and the fire at our center rises
with drum, rattle and chant.

Before me the noble beauty of Gaia,
jeweled in her cloak of deep space,
is undiminished by passing events:
I see streaks of fire, storm and war,
drought, flood and city squalls.
Tears slide down my cheeks,
fall into my hands.
She is the oldest soul among us
and onto her glowing red wounds
I pour blue liquid light to cool her,
place green poultices for healing.

I pray over broken places,
add to the love imbued
within her seas and lands,
add to the love each living being
carries for our remarkable spaceship,
the only home we know.

We once knew who we were,
knew the great SHE:
we can know again.

Mark Young

vacation 2022

desperate starfish cling to the backside
of rocks jutting from the ocean, battered
by waves as relentless as today's news

black mussels cemented to the stones
welcome the incessant crash of brine
tiny meals snagged by the jagged shells

crabs skitter past anemones, snails scoot
across the ebony sand, seagulls scavenge
and squawk, seashells lie abandoned

my granddaughter clutches my hand, her
eyes full of wonder, absorbed in the moment
and lightly squeezes her fingers around mine

while on the horizon, fog rolls in, and will soon
hide the cool brightness of the Sonoma afternoon
but for now, I, too, am filled with awe.

BLAZE

Alicia Kimberly

Matthew 24:6

Wars, and rumors of war–
see that you be not troubled;
all these things must come
to pass, but the end is not–
yet, here it is, as it's always
been–two hands drawn
across a table, each thrusting
their tumbler toward the other's.

A missile falls on a hospital
where deafened ears breathe
countless final sighs in the silent,
split-second between the crystal
clink of the glass rims
and the crinkle-eyed sláinte.

We know how it is, has always
been–see the overturned truck's
cracked windshield in the ditch,
moments before we pull into
our driveways, carry our sleepy
little ones upstairs to their beds,
wash our faces.

We know, then, because we saw
the blue lights, the stretcher,
refused to meet Azrael's
shrouded gaze, eyes dead fixed
on the road ahead, white-knuckle
gripped our steering wheels,
floored the pedal to clear
the swing of his scythe.

I measure-mark my daughter's height

on her bedpost. A man in a prison
jumpsuit tallies another sun-rotation on his.
Uriel abandons his guard of the garden
to go inspect doorways for lamb's blood,
discarding his flaming weapon.
The city of angels catches fire.
Or maybe it was just a cigarette
still burning, thrown into a bush.
The fox fleeing the inferno
doesn't give a damn how it began.
Thousands of men fall

on a blood-soaked beach,
four miles away a farmer slits
his hog's throat, his wife jars
sweet, red, sticky jams.
A woman and a cat both give birth
on different floors of the same cottage.
The runt of the litter doesn't make it.
Despair, her mother eats the corpse.

In the backyard, two children
exchange love notes on a swing-set.
Michael's fingers close
around his sword. We
desperately try to learn not to worry
about how it is, how it's always been.

the walls

while lightning
knowing its cap
ties to absolute ground

alabaster becomes
the moan of moon

picture the walls
as facing mirrors

twenty-two-thousand years
and fire now

the melting night
a fixture then

fixed-face to thought
in
and not at
a surround

the walls of history

Carol Tahir

Summer to Fall

Grains of sand clump on the beach
after a wave washes over.
Sand crabs burrow into moist silica,
hide from pails and shovels.
Salt water anglers cast their lines
hoping to catch the evening meal.
Sunset bonfires crackle in the twilight;
BBQ fish roasting in a bed of veggies.

Music and dancing under stars,
frolicking beachgoers gather in circles,
celebrate through summer solstice
and the beginning of Autumn Equinox.

Crisp air with a nip of chill.
Apples scent the breezes.
Warm cider, powdered sugar doughnuts,
mustaches of white after one bite.
The trees undress after summer parties,
leave colors strewn along the way,
harbinger of coming winter's sleep
after late summer bonfires.

The key of wait

crowning myself
with sifted sun
(softening light)
i am the neck of Modigliani
mirrored to sound

to self's half-door
if sound is blue
and challenges
are the key of wait

where are Soutine's deep reds
almond seeds reflected
on whose waistcoat
and where are the women-priests
of cardinal De Kooning's sass
unfolding the fins of my solid day

where are Rembrandt's selfies

a single hair
on the new page
distracts crossing
curves so slightly
curves to itself

i've fallen on read
not to be blown off

Tanya Whitney

The Storm

Blackened skies as dark as night,
Rolling clouds of rain and wind
Threaten all in its path
With death and destruction.

Blackened skies as dark as night
Illuminated with white flashes of light,
Booming with a thundering roar,
Passes across stormy sky.

Blackened skies as dark as night
Weep upon the landscape
With teardrops of rain,
Purge with refreshing waters.

Blackened skies as dark as night
Move on to another place and time,
Leave brightened skies and landscapes
Revitalized from the tempests.

CChristy White

I want to touch you--

      when lightning leaps
            across tempestuous skies
        the first charge builds
    humming from the storm
            with a concentrated
bolt
      streaming through mountainous clouds
                dives
to the ground

      and a tree of light is born

too bright to see
    details of leaves and twigs
          as branches burn
              the trunk
balances
on stone and dirt   sends
           hot roots into the
ground
    water dances with the currents
    and the afterimage
            glows in your eyes

Umar O. Abdul

Mosquitoes in my village

Mosquitoes in my village
come with large kegs
hanging across their shoulders
like soldiers with a shield,
and a long straw in their hands
as a soldier holds his sword.
As they approach, they sing
The songs of warriors.

Mosquitoes in my village
make no friends.
They force swords into my skin
and draw their share of blood
until their kegs are filled.

Even as I applaud
the mosquitoes in my village,
I loathe them. Their goal
is to steal my spirit.

Alicia Kimberly

Heart

If I could fold myself like paper,
origami love note to tuck, secure
into your pocket, or ventricle,
wrap us both inside every blanket,
by every fireplace in the entire world,
bind all the stars by their gleaming
light into your golden hair, it might,
not quite but almost be enough.
Instead I gather your tiny hand
in mine, let the faint squeeze
of flushed skin fill me, let my chest
burst open, and roar with the excess.

Jack Evans

Peggy's Blue Skylight

Winter crashes into night
Pale light washes over the bed
She slips from under sheets
Her flesh by Botticelli
Her hair like platinum heat
Thoughts linger through fractured hours
Light cracks the surface
Time spills from muted walls
Her hand retraces magic

A taxi races through a downpour of traffic
The stormy sounds of Charles Mingus
Rages in her waking blood

Mark Young

Dinner With My Brother at Zarda BBQ

You have to eat,
even on death watch
he said, sauce smiling
from his mouth to his ears.
Slathered ribs and onion rings,
beans and coleslaw,
no room to lay meatless bones.
A pitcher of Coors Light.
A handful of napkins.

I poured a beer.

What we gonna do when she dies,
I mean, with the stuff in the house?
I want the red chair.
I need the computer desk
and the curtains in the living room,
my wife likes the silver bracelet
dad gave her for their anniversary.
What do you want?

Another beer, I said.
I refilled my glass,
pushed aside my food.

I wanted to get drunk.

I wanted to drive Matchbox cars
down roads smoothed in summer dust,
past giant green army men --
mine sweepers, radio operators,
angry soldiers with rifles raised
prepared to pierce their enemies
with plastic bayonets.
I wanted my father to come home,

carrying his black lunch pail,
cuffs of his pants rolled up,
Pall Mall ashes defying gravity.
I wanted to play catch with him
squatting like Johnny Bench
beside the white meadowsweet,
to feel the sizzle of his fastball
pound my mitt and then
to sit with him on the porch swing
as he showed me how to oil my glove,
wrap it around a baseball.
slip it under my pillow and sleep
on it, force the pocket
into the shape I wanted.

Cynthia Hogue

To Hide a Child
            (France 1941/2012)

1

Who's speaking, please?
It no longer matters.

Who else knew?
No one we trusted, no one.

Was the child small enough
to fit in a cupboard?

*One day before soldiers came,
the child* sauvage *arrived*

from the blue horizon, hungry.
Did the child look foreign?

What does foreign
look like to you?

2

How could a child travel alone?
*Not the child but the wild apples
in the fields along the lanes
past our house were our business:*

*to collect them in season,
to make the tart sauce
for pork in fall.* Did you
hide this child out of guilt?

The child was in danger

from us, *unmoved,*
gazing out our window.
Did you embellish this story?

3

Children harried, rounded up,
and worse, there, then,
as here, now?

Why not close the blinds
to soaring poplars, their glossy
leaves and populated shadows?

We happened to be
looking hard and at last
saw that the child's danger

cracks ajar the door
we thought protected us
 let the light in.

rpt. From *Field*

Kenneth Weene

You the earth, I the plower

Perhaps a sip—
        or just a swallow—
                bitter,
                sweet,
                salt and sorrow.
Our kiss will linger for the moment—
        a scent of jasmine,
                a smell of flowers.
A gentle stir in the stillest nights
        caresses,
                touches—
                        the touch excites.
The wine is strong,
        confused the hour;
before our love
        I have no power.
The bottom land is lying fallow,
and tempered rain may well yet shower.
We'll plant the seed of our tomorrow;
        you the earth,
                        I the plower.

damp map to a small place

at best summer waits
its call approximates
from bearded tablecloths

        a mad crowd
        a single's set
        and greasy plates

one bedroom at back
lacks combination
while the slender woman moves soundless

        in a long straight dress
           an unmade bed
           a lidless toilet

where is love without a dog
slip-lace with a frayed hem
bras unnecessary
walking-- waking-- waiting

        better bitter
        bare to the foot

kitchen faces are soft-salt coins
curling surfaces while fingering please
orchard in the city's only name

        climate uncontrolled
        a cola bottle tunnel
        no elbows

summer is also backyard toys
naked in predawn dew

        a hurt of extra heat
        a dried frog
licenses for cankerous street carnivals
        someone may notice particulars

where there is not enough evidence
to deter the endless scams of games
no Michelangelo gracing creations
                              monkey business
                              mania
                 and a small place for fun

Susan Vespoli

Flagstaff, She Is on Fire

And then another forest fire. *Pipeline,* after *Haywire,*
Tunnel, and *Double.* Orange sun hangs in blue-haze bruised
sky. University town where I birthed and nursed two babies,

finished my fricking bachelor's degree at 28. My then-husband
had said, *no you can't,* and I'd said, *watch me.* Got a paper route,
I swear, walked streets with one kid in an umbrella stroller, cloth
sack

slung over my shoulder, *Arizona Daily Suns* stuck in plastic tubes
for tuition money. Mountains, ski runs, deer roaming Buffalo
Park. Today there are plumes of smoke, Hotshot crews buying

cantaloupe and gummies at the Safeway, tanker trucks, skeleton
trees
and a melted cell phone tower on Hwy 89. Evacuees with suitcases.
Fences down, paper signs posted: *Thank you, First Responders*;

the whole town is under a cloud of soot and aftermath. Sandbags
line roads. Flood predictions. An air of dread or fear. Hair on fire.

Mark Young

A Dozen (or so) Pieces of Sage Advice from an
Upper-Middle-Aged Man Who May or May Not
Have Experienced Many of the Things Suggested
Below.

Never mosh with your family on a descending elevator
        if you expect to attend the Blue Man Group show on time.

Never play ding-dong ditch'em in the pouring rain. Mud craters
        make the escape difficult and your car interior disgusting.

Never play that game when it's icy, either. When you flee
        a nervous foot on the gas pedal could kill you.

Never use WebMD.

Never trust an agent who books your R&B band in Dodge City
        at a club that features a mechanical bull.

Also, never accept a gig in Huron, South Dakota, until you know
        if the walls of the club have cracks that leak sunshine.

Never jump in the deep end of the pool wearing steel-toed
        boots. You're not that good a swimmer.

Never lend to a friend and expect to get what you're owed.
        Give it to them and plan on them just being moochy.

Never buy a bake sale pie.

In the midst of a midnight snowstorm, never drive
        a '72 Maverick down an abandoned road.

And never trust your passenger to hitchhike to town and send
        help, especially if they are a jerk who will just go to bed.

Never light up a cigarette in front of your religious girlfriend.

It causes stress, anxiety, and eventual loneliness.

Never drink martinis alone on your patio until you start to bawl.

Or do them all.

Alicia Kimberly

For All the Universe

1.

For all the universe, and your whirling
swirling great spheres of exploding gaslight
who, by design, or more likely, chance
saw fit to illuminate in this millisecond
the ever sandcastle-crumbling and refilling
celestial hourglass my grain of stardust falls
through, diving into a double helix set ablaze
with wonder, my entire weight in gratefulness
far too faint for your notice–I know, I've seen
in pictures, how the small blue sphere veils
itself in white, lights up from far away.
Down here on the crust, my boots
made from the stretched skin of dead
things kick up tiny dust clouds,
these creatures you made me of,
put me into, are better suited
to searching than praise, anyway.

2.

When we look, we find tiny stone statues
under centuries of mudslides, pyramids
under oceans, decide that centuries is a long time.
We must be your jesters. We tell you stories
of angels, demons, aliens, lifting our hands
to the starry skies for them, imagining
that our souls could become unpinned
from our mother's giant, spinning, beautiful corpse.
She whispers to me that all the wondrous
monuments will burn to nothing, laughing,
no heaven nor hell, no anything, infinite.
She told me life is more precious this way–

a mortal coil unwinding, then springing back
with such speed that the atoms undo themselves,
disintegrate particles, Adam returned to dust,
the pleasure intensified in the rarity of a single
apple to a man who's been starved
and will be sent out to starve again,

3.

but I'd rather be well fed.
How many life spans would it take to drive
every highway, walk every town square,
sit every holy place, commune with the lifetimes
of ghosts who've prayed there, to touch
and taste every living thing, to hold my children
until I am sated of my need to hold them?
Yet how much of me dies everyday,
constantly trimmed off the top, spat out
into my coffee cup, sloughed off the heel,
fallen out of my head in the shower?
Shedding the cells that make me constantly
just enough, steady, so as not to become a tumor
—but oh! That secret part that would make
endless love to you, universe, that wishes
this weedling cancer, this me, would cover
this whole world over, could grow forever.

Rosemarie Dombrowski

Good and Bad

My therapist sends me a link
to *cognitive distortions.*
A former student inquires
about my son.
I use the phrase *psychotic episode*
twice in one day.

My friend with Parkinson's
has passed away.
My mother is scattered
and growing fearful of cars.

I tell my former lover
that my body is a container for pain,
that pain is a kind of sadness
that lives deep inside us,
like how our days can be
two things at the same time,
the flame and the darkness.

Fire Season Again

what is it now
        third   fourth
wave: to say goodbye
      with empty hands
      :water coming to shore
      : body surfs   shivers

this wave a firestorm
      takes everything
time measured in tragedy
      too much
      too many
         too quick

tears trace losses
in ashes in hiss
      of breathing machines
too many trees
      losing count

beg a god
      or the doctor
no bargains
no hugs
      circle names
      I used to know

black is burn
      is formal clothing
      mask below water eyes
         foundations crack
         with heat
another wave comes

who can breathe

          so much ash   white
sheets of it
hospital cornered

forests of smoke
                    too quiet

EMBERS

Alicia Kimberly

Ark

1

In the sultry-misted darkness of those ancient nights, pre-flooded,
great winged sons of the Word drifted from golden plane to glide,
skirt, virtue itself scattered thin 'cross sea and shore-sand angels,

bent for singular purpose, to make of the daughters of men
their whore-wives, conceive something new in their wombs,
and in that act of generation, make creator-gods of themselves.

The women, more ape than angel, brought forth to them giants too big
to be borne; the reward for their labor ragged-rip, rent. To this offspring,
a gift from their fathers—enlightenment beyond their evolution.

2

With this knowledge the children built. Dwellings for themselves
of toxic chemical compounds; filled the homecages with cameras
to monitor them—to take the place of their forgotten grandfather,

the ever-watching Word—who'd grown an unholy leaden resentment
one teaspoonful at a time—broke His dams when He saw them build
a nuclear bomb. He let it pour, an ever-swallowing deluge of sea.

Prometheus' punishment was too good for His errant sons,
He unleashed His champion, Michael, to find them out, bind
them, in the dark. The children of men, sentenced to drown.

3

Railing in vain against catastrophe, homosapien mothers wove
enormous baskets of papyrus, pitch-bathed, in which to float
their babies through the endless devour— the coming electricity

storm, the tides growing ever-higher as the ice-mountains cracked,
melted like frostbitten volcanoes pooling around ankles of demi-
gods
in suits, caught up in, consumed by their own battle, blind to all
else.

These mothers, priestess all, accomplished Wonder, unsinkable
cloisters swimming alongside each-other, atlantic schools filled
with miracles–Moses, Sargon, Karna, Romulus and Remus.

4

But the tar-filled warhearts of those who resented anyone owning
even a basket-full of hope, opened themselves, seeped their vile
sludge down their arms, formed into their hands, a weapon.
They riddled the sacred children with bullet holes.

In fervent prayer-dreams, the frenzy-most yearn of my marrow,
I rescue them all; the children of men lapping at the waves,
tears bleeding the salt-water crimson, and saltier still,

but my own daughters are treading water, two tremble-terrified
flesh-of-my-flesh saline pillars who deserve an olympic ocean
liner. I have a rusted handsaw, and the blueprints for a dinghy.

5

Always the end of days in the anxious minds of those who came
before me, they built for these times a safehouse, a wooden ark;
heavy-laden with milk and honey, music, poetry, nitroglycerin.

My ancestors' ghosts still dwell inside, they stand, laughing,
gazing, smoking on the deck. They don't like it when I leave.
The agents drag me back, trussed, for my own safety. I bite.

I scream for my children to leave me and run. It'll go up,
it'll go up, any minute now. Ash-embers fly, helterskelter,
tiny stars falling to land on the still-dry wood.

Mark Young

Morning Delivery

Sundays my father rose early,
dressed while the sky was still onyx
and with knobby hands that ached from
blue-collar labor, rolled heavy
newspapers bulging with inserts
of groceries and furniture,
and loud comics. No one thanked him.

I would wake and hear the cold snap
of rubber bands, smell the Pall Mall
smoke and the Folgers coffee. He'd
call, and slowly I would rise and
dress, dreading the chill reception.

He would trudge to the curb through snow
and the gray of winter mornings
wearing his black work shoes - they were
 all he had - start up the Ford Fairlane
so I could stay warm as we drove
through the neighborhood tossing bad
news and meager ads on porches.
Not much was said. Never thank you.

After the papers were cast out
after he smoked six cigarettes,
we would stop at the store for glazed
donuts. Every week. For five years.
And what did I know? What did I
know of the selfish assumptions
of a nine-year-old and the mum
love of a parent's blossomed heart.

Kenneth Weene

Paper Sack

My grandmother used a deconstructed
paper sack. It might once have held
potatoes or boxes of macaroni
and cheese and bread
to fill empty stomachs.

She wrapped that craft brown paper
around ideas—sketched in black skinny
-tipped felt marker—folded neatly,
small pressed rectangles
slipped into the bottom dresser drawer.

There is place for everything
even thoughts—especially thin-lined
thoughts left unpuzzled for grandchildren
to find and wonder
what the world might have been,

those poems about her unknown love.
After the war, when he didn't return,
grandmother married. There's a photograph,
him stern, her mournful
She was never supposed to shed tears

    —for all that she had lost.

CChristy White

What Will the Dead Say?

A bright gold sun with bells
hangs on my blue front door.
Every movement shivers
bells into tinkling voices.
Now the dead can enter,
speak to me, but first
I have to learn Ukraine,
maybe Russian, Arabic
and Congolese as well.
They will speak slow,
stumble-tongued,
because languages
are fading from memory.
Their new life stories
we may not understand,
yet in time, like our mothers,
they may speak in the voice of Angel,
or perhaps the voice of love.
Can we all learn that language
before our bodies fall silent
into fire and dust?
For now, they are asking me
to listen, to pretend I comprehend;
I turn my face away as words
filter through grief.

John Daleiden

I don't care if I never get back
Solo *Renhai* on the theme of
memorable moments in
baseball

1. How sweet it is . . .

buying me
peanuts and Cracker Jack—
an ivy clad wall

the umpire shouting, "Play ball"—
Babe rounding third to home

the scent of hotdogs—
for it's one, two, three strikes,
you're out

2. I Remember . . .

Harry Caray
calling a play-by-play game—
the rise to the mound

stealing from base to base—
the sharp, slapping of leather

a loud, whizzing bunt
passing the shortstop—
two-base hit

3. Through the Seasons . . .

one hundred eight years
without a championship—
windy city

a westward expansion—
Brooklyn Dodgers' LA move

Marianne Moore,
poet, slamming a home run—
front page news

4. Batter up . . .

scoreboard: 3 to 2
at the bottom of the ninth—
clouds in a blue sky

the umpire calling, "Ball four—"
roaring from the grandstand

"get red-hots here—"
motionless, the batter
striking the third out"

Cynthia Hogue

Instead it is dark
(1944-2018)

I woke to the dead
and was among them.

how this happened,
who did this to us

unaccountably
hatred glosses

and evidence belies.
ourselves but ourselves.

I'd gone to the corner
when the bakery opened,

mouthing regards
to a rare sun, then suddenly –

though not – I remember
nothing else.

I feel around me now
and everyone's near

who waited for bread
or God one morning.

it's true I thought at the last
I heard something but didn't think

to turn, nor catch sight of,
nor glean time to.

Rpt. from *Kestrel*

Facebook Post

Last I looked, she is married:
happy, two children,
husband middle management,
not a rhyme or verse in his body;
reliable, somebody who'll help
pay the children's college—
degrees in engineering or business—
with no remarking or scandal.

Last time I looked—was it six
or five hours since—
almost every day
I look to see what she's posted,
what I've missed of her life
while editing my own;
avoiding wasted words like
I love you.

I wish we could go back
to high school prom
drinking grape juice and vodka
not asking about the rest
of our lives. Waking next
day in a copse of alder and bramble.
I wrote a poem, which
I've never had the chance to read.

Jack Evans

The Sadness of Time Passing

Ozu understood it
And Tarkovsky and
Bergman
The melancholy of moments
The indiscernible madness
Of silence
The swift passage of
Irretrievable seconds
Lost forever to
The looking glass of mystery
Held only inside of memory and
Forever being altered
By the editing
Of light

Alicia Kimberly

2 Kings 9:33-37

Listen for the chariot, always faced
down to cold concrete, eyes avoid
everyone who can read the red letter
on my breast, the one that hangs
off the licked lips of English professors
and unbuttoned police uniform-shirts,
cell-door-clang memories that make me
want to vomit into the shoes I stole
from the second-hand store, back when
I lived at the bus stop on Tuesdays.

Princess of the Phoenician gutter--
bake-on mud, blood-cake foot-soles,
abomination is not the legacy I wanted
to leave my daughters. If not for them,
I'd've kept burning the bull I rode naked
through town squares, drunk on choler
toward your god; dead-set on fulfilling
his ancient prophecy that I'd die
worth nothing without his approval.

Where've you gone, Elijah?
I'd like to cut a deal.
Fire's dying down on Carmel,
I can feel their incisors;
dogs' tongues begin to brush my bones,
soft, still, small.

Rosemarie Dombrowski

Poetry Therapy at the Maricopa Reentry Center, Week 4

It began with a beautiful spring day.

It reminded me of *Bullet in the Brain,*
the final electrical impulse before dying,
the protagonist's little league dreams.
A baseball game has always been
a symbol of innocence.

In Dominic's poem,
the center fielder is stabbed
by multiple assailants.
Everyone remains fixed in their position –
on the diamond, in the outfield,
on the bench –
until the choppers touch down
and extract the body.

He ends it there.
It doesn't matter what happened next.

Cynthia Hogue

After the War There Was No Food

As a boy the man dreamed he lay in a box
of mineral salts, ruby, amber, quartz-clear.

He imagined eating the raw meat
of the goat whose milk he sucked as newborn.

Death was his mother, match-thin
and unsmiling. He loved her fiercely,

voraciously
bleating into her sad face as he nursed.

Starving, the boy grew tall but not straight,
so lean the wind might sweep him off.

Lately, the man returned to the Forêt de Chinon,
which did not comfort him,

so many trees harvested
he lost his way. Hunger

was all he'd known when
a long time ago he pleaded

for Death his mother
to feed him. He bent to touch

himself because, after all,
Death would not.

Rpt. from *Field*

Umar O. Abdul

Lullaby

Sleep, oh young people, sleep.
When you wake up, play hide and seek,
run round the palm trees,
then go back again to sleep.

Now, rain drops drum the roof;
the soil is too wet to be tilled.
So, sleep and dream your dreams.

The past has cultivated your land
and the palm fruits are ripe.
They provide enough oil for papa's yam.
No need to work yourself lame.
So, sleep and forget.

Sleep, oh young people, sleep.
Does tomorrow matter?
Your yesterday is now gone
and today is tomorrow's yesterday.
Just sleep and dream your dreams.

Dream the biggest dreams.
Are your mamas and papas not here?
Will they not stay forever to fill
The mouths they made with milk?
So, sleep and forget.

Sleep, oh young people, sleep.
Keep your eyes closed and do not fret;
everything is taken care.
When the dawn of dark becomes dusk.

Kenneth Weene

The ghosts were running late last night
                     and so I fell to sleep;
but then they caught up with me and met me in my dreams.
Call them furies, poltergeists, or demons of the night;
they torment me for all my sins from dark until dawn's light.

In the days I can recall the joys and loves that I have known;
but when the light fades away, I suffer until dawn—
remembering the sorrows; recollecting all the fears.
My dreams replete with sighs and cries; my nights complete with
tears.

Memory, that torturer, reminds me of the wrongs that I have done;
and then increases suffering by recalling things undone.
The visions of might-have-beens and those I fear that were:
I regret all those sins and my true repentance I aver.

But were I to live once more, and would it mean your love to keep
I must admit of all those sins I now repent of having sown
I would repeat though into hell I know my soul be plunged.
Better to be by Satan judged than never having by you been loved.

Charles Watts

Harmony
      In the voice of Margo Fish
      on her 90th

The deck needs a coat of urethane
The forest floor needs raking
Because it is my garden

I need to top the tallest trees
So I can see the mountains again

The dock needs a few new boards
And a pontoon or two to keep it floating

The dog needs a haircut because
Well, he looks just like my dog should
I'll take care of that later

Friends are coming for dinner
Again. Everyone I love
Becomes my husband or wife or child
And everyone I meet is invited

Please stay and make some music
Bring your drawings or
Say your poems or dance
With me on these ash blond floors

Tell me why you are different
And why it doesn't matter

Everything is fine until it isn't
So let's play now
While we can

Alicia Kimberly

Bifröst

Only say, a billion galaxies, I can't count higher,
come and gone--and how many intelligences
evolved just enough, to ask why they had, merely
to perish in ignorant darkness of cosmic rupture;
hands lifted to their dying sun's disintegration,
believing they stood alone in a universe abandoned
by some story-told creator. At the sheer thought
I shudder all over, uncontrollable shivering at my
ponderous insignificance as I trundle up the stair-
case carpet on stiff ankles which used to dance
in orbit on wooden boards before they were broken.

I find my consequence in the spot
my daughter has fallen asleep
on the floor, limp brown hair tangled in
the glasses she's forgotten to take off,
again. I untwist the snarls, delicate,
lift the spectacles with anxious fingertips,
so she wont wake, so the plastic frames
won't bruise the sacred, celestial bridge
between her eyes and mine.

ASHES

Mark Young

Take Me Home

I've had enough my mother said, leaning over
her nursing home bed, packing a suitcase
set on sheets spotted with pin-prick blossoms of red.

Take me home, take me home, where I can salt
my potatoes and salve my wounds, where dad
will return from under the earth or the skies overhead.

He'll scale the trellis to the bedroom, his sleeves rolled
up past his anchor tattoo and carry me away from stacks
of waste; bills & newspapers, cards & letters, B&W photos,

a life I don't remember as my own.

Comb my hair, honey, so I'll look good for him,
wash my face and fetch my teeth, powder a tawny base,
disguise my wrinkles, color my lips with cinnamon wine.

Find the rose dress from the cedar chest, the black
high heels that pinch my toes, open my jewelry box
and unravel the bracelet he bought, rub away the tarnish

from the silver heads of the children. I am ready to go,
please bring my ring, slip it on my finger,
and sit me near the window.

Alicia Kimberly

Five-o'clock

There's a lite-heavy September-type
feeling around five-o'clock, just as blue
and white clouds dim-merge, dissolving
into soft gray monosky, daytime faded
red signs pop-off tomato, and greenery
explodes punches to the gut, shoots
theatric between the eyes, blasts blacktop
mountain highway corner, swerving
lightning-yellow lines across the horizon.

A happy-sad that drags on like the week
between Christmas and New Years lasts
an hour or two every evening. A grasping
on to the frayed end of a tug-o-war rope,
the second-to-last chapter of an easy-read
novel or final season of a favorite television
series, anticipation flickering come-home
street lights from the kickball diamond.

Butter-fluttering eyelashes in the last
stanza of bedtime lullaby-and-kisses,
hugs by the front door, shrugging on coats,
gripping the minutes like grandad's cane
handle as the heavy-heart chest-clock
explodes bright before the short hand
strikes the darkening into night.

Kenneth Weene

Nous avons le cafard
      (we have the blues)

how she endures
when survival is decision
and will
        that marvelous power
                                within
move your foot   it cries
        now the other   and again

where was mother
when you learned to walk
across the room   street   years
that long stretch until
you're home again
and the billows of sea
gone still blue as the satin pillow

an oak coffin
        why we didn't settle for pine

she went after he died
disappeared from us   from herself
living someplace in her failing head
curled back   breast to knees
waiting   waiting to be born again
fetal thumb suck
        heart beat

they use feeding tubes
        she requires a nipple   formula

in maternity a woman screams
        a stillborn's loss
would she lie now   near death

       offer her untouched
             tumescent breast

being scurries
through tunnels of light
through eternity's subways

the old woman curled in pain
       waits again for palsy's end
           for the train to arrive

an oak coffin
       why we didn't settle for pine

Cynthia Hogue

The Pacifist

War
was
wasteland,
was a way
of putting it.

Loud boombadaboom of the bombs.
Sometimes distant sometimes close.
Each moment asplinter a spark a birth.
Each person a singular globe until
out, out—

No pigs left we did not eat pork.
No cows we did not drink milk.No chickens we did not boil
eggs.

What did we eat I do not remember
eating. Or not eating.

I remember washing maybe once a month maybe once a year.
I wasn't happy or sad neither clean nor unclean.
Mother washing sheets in the stream out back.
Mother selling the rabbit weren't there more we could eat?
Rabbit's dear.

War's a way of living not living.
Question it doesn't matter it's just war always called *the*
just war. I saw through words used to just-
ify war as if glass sharpening sunlight into fire.
I was forever on fire.

Rpt. from *Cutthroat*

CChristy White

The Falling Wife

after The Falling Soldier, photo
by Robert Capa, 1936, Spanish Civil War

The moment I fell senseless,
the ground beneath became liquid,
everything felt changed.
My mother, my companions, twittered
around me, a flight of larks
disturbed with unknowing.
All faded like a darkening stage
and I was above him on that hill
where he lay still, rifle dropped,
arms out as if to embrace
the spirit I had become.
A light rose up from him
as a shadow overtook me
and I returned to myself
looking into an azure sky
empty of cloud or wavering leaf,
broken with absolute knowledge.

Jimmy Broccoli

A Detuned Piano Reminds Me of Her Sadness

I listen to the sounds of a detuned piano on the radio, and the music
is exquisite -
It reminds me of her beauty and of her sadness

Angelic, yet brief, thoughts of her unfold before me...

Her dramatic, well-tailored silhouette towers lovingly in the room's
dim light
While sitting on the couch, I stare at the back of her elegant, tight-
fitting dress
She stares out the window, poetically, into the darkness
Then, turns her head around to smile at me
She is an enchanting evening – lit, flickering candles and glasses of
fine wine

She moves, gently, almost floating, drifting charmingly to sit beside
me
Soft music embraces the room, dancing delicately and affectionately
around us
Her melancholy twinkles, like declining stars before their final
performance
She leans into me, her perfume capturing the brilliance of autumn
memories
I sense her closing her eyes, tenderly and enduringly – and I do not
move

Her opulent stillness takes a bow, the audience applauds in
appreciation and her heartbeat slows
The evening begins to weep, and it will weep forever

Tonight, I listen to the sounds of a detuned piano on the radio
And think of nothing other than of her beauty and of her sadness

Charles Watts

When Her Body Died

When her body died
All that was left
Were pictures in the mind
On paper in fading albums
Or stored in the cloud

A summer day
Carrying her last newborn
Up the steps to
Her mother's house

Standing on tiptoe
Hands at the top
Of a propeller
Pulling it down
To start the biplane's engine

Parallel to the water
Just off the diving board
Before a tuck and roll
Into the pool

My brother and I
Went to see her
Before the cremation
Not our mother behind the glass
But an unwrapped mummy
Awaiting the flame

Eyes closed, she is running
Out of the dark tunnel
Into the light

Charles Watts

Death Watch

Morphine drip oxygen tubes
Each breath an origami crane
Floating silently across the room
Her body the last rough-hewn beam
From an ancient barn that has seen
One too many winters

Children gathered to handhold
The last moment together
One last stitch in the quilt
Of her days

           a husband
Too proud to cry and not
Able to say his goodbyes
In the presence of others

But there, as always, there
In the shadows, grief unspoken
Each broken heartbeat
An origami crane
Floating silently across the room

CChristy White

If Steve…

… had been a young man today
struggling to understand his broken self,
he would be dead in that dirty bathroom
in the rundown motel out near West Van Buren
because a psychotic break and rampaging paranoia
caused him to sit on the cold tile shivering in fear
and embrace an empty handgun.
(I like to think it was empty, but maybe not…
my own memory is incomplete and broken.)
He was sure drug dealers were out for his blood
so why wouldn't he also think the policemen
who waited outside his room were the same?
But that was 1978, and when those police
encountered a crazy man with a gun,
their first impulse was not to shoot, but to talk
until he put the gun down, came out of the bathroom,
and agreed to self-commit to the psychiatric hospital.
The police called me, told me about my brother,
and it was a terrible moment, but he survived.
I can work with being alive.

Kenneth Weene

listening to Messiaen September, 2020

Making sense is overrated
better the gibberings of mad men.
Address the homeless;
tell them the latest statistics
fresh from randomization.
As long as there is measurement
science requires no sanity.
Reassure those who peddle nonsense,
who call politicians friends.
Keep tally, take careful inventory.
Talk about the missing;
the counting by definition
will add together in the end.
Double entry each atrocity.
Tabulate the records of the dead.
Civilization has grown no wiser;
we cannot stop the plague of men.
Carefully keep track
and give number to the dead.

Nous sommes tous condamnés.

We are all doomed.

Alicia Kimberly

I Wrote My First Poem About You.

How old were we, eleven, twelve? Just two children
kissing behind my garage, between the bee-infested
pear tree and the conifer the owl lived in, the grass
covered in May morning frost and littered with rabbit
ears, limbs, and smelled of wild things, rain, and you,
pink-cheeked little boy. Our eyes open, wide-green,
your white-gold curls dripped on my freckled nose
like a colander of cellentani and your mouth was full
of America-colored orthodontic bands and my long
brown braids entwined silent secrets made of winking,
twinkling hope that I wouldn't see you any less often,
despite the moving truck being filled in the driveway.

You'd broken my heart twice-over by the time I'd realized
I loved you. I did sleep the night you kissed another girl-
child in front of our friends, in front of me, but I tossed
in my blankets. I wet-smudged the pillow with fourteen
year old tears, I had a fantastical dream in which I threw
myself over a waterfall and drowned, and then, smiling,
watched you dress in a beautiful black suit, watched you
carry flowers to my funeral.

We laughed at ourselves on the internet later, at our drama-
tic delusions–those of grandeur, of having a real significance
to anyone other than our own children.

It's been twenty years.
I can't look at the photo
that your wife sent me.

Cheeks so thin and gray,
the awful tube in your chest.

this time, death is not.

A dream.

Tanya Whitney

Absolution in Limbo

You asked for the one thing
I could not freely provide.
Our actions on that day
forever changed two lives.

Hurtful words were spoken,
shouted at one another,
have tarnished and tainted
all hope of reconciliation.

We never thought it would end
this way in a sea of tears and anger.
Both of us knew that it was
all beyond repairing the trust.

Maybe in time, the pain will
cease to tear our hearts in two.
Fond memories will overshadow
the pain and sorrow of that day.

Only then would we really mean
what needs to be said to each other.
Maybe then the harsh words can be
forgiven and our regrets ring true.

Adamu Ibrahim Mohammed

Suicide

Insects deserve insecticides
for preying on the souls of our plants;
Snappy application of sniper; insects' souls wiper

Have we done ourselves this doom?
Is this sniper our suicide's tool?

We have chosen the hangman's rope by our hands.
Either by the ballot or secret bailout
We have traded our national hope
for a pot of soup

When we had hope
We forgot the hangman's noose and take a dive for
crumbs on politician's table

Little did we know that we need life to stay alive.

With Strings Attached

You can't love me with strings attached
to my arms, feet, shoulders, knees and head.
You can't hold me in mid-air
and play me, show me off to your friends
for their amusement and your own pleasure,
you the magician who works wonders and gets the applause.

You can't love me with strings attached
that I must react the way you push and pull
on the strings,
or blame me for your hands on the stick not working properly
by throwing a fit – and me – into the bottom of a closet
with the other discarded toys and dolls,
because you hate me and want to forget
by closing the closet door and leaving us in darkness.

You can't love me with strings attached,
get lonely and bored all alone in the room of your life
then say you'll open the door, pick me up again and play –
but this time I better behave right
better keep you happy this time, because I know my place
whether out in the open or behind closed doors.

No. You can't love me with strings attached.
It's not just that I am not a toy,
this declaration of humanity.
Neither can you treat yourself like a child.
You cannot love a person like a toy – with strings attached.

Rosemarie Dombrowski

Poetry Therapy at the Maricopa Reentry Center, Week 28

We set our secrets on fire
in the pit that Carl built.
It seemed fitting to say his name
as we were burning our shame.

I keep my list vague
in case we can't get them lit,
in case we get caught by C.O.s.

I leave my radio in the classroom,
my visitor's badge too.
My practices are irresponsible.
I trust too many of them.
I embrace them too often.
I carry their burdens
when they leave.

Earnest A. Shoemate

The Paperback

Faded and creased the man
Cover gently closed
A wave of sadness
On the warn face
Old friends parting
Memories made
From ancient pages

Time had ravaged both
Used for support
Man and book once
Leveled a kitchen table
Raised a family
Imparted knowledge
When well and able

It held a universe
Of other's dreams
Realms of visions
Once perceived
One who shared
His secret thoughts
Friend he may have been

It had cost him
Fifty cents
The dogeared pages
Yellowed paper
Contemplation
Toss away
Or conflagration

Did not let loose
That ancient tome
He and it had

Shared a home
That old old book
At rest once more
Waited

They searched
Quietly in that
The silent house
What to save
If anything
The sentiment
That it could bring

Serious faces worn
Hushed and whispered
Hearts were torn
That book rose once again
Within the hands of
A dark-haired boy
Who wore his grandpa's grin

Mark Young

Imagine

sitting on a porch swing
next to five-year-old
You, jeans muddy after
his search for earth
worms. Dime-store tennis
shoes dangle below his
cuffed pants, soaked
and filthy from the day's
adventure. The child pours
out stories of the day,
drinks a grape Fanta,
exuberant about the bucket
of bait at his side. Imagine
you muss his crewcut,
see his brown eyes
unclouded by burdens
of overdue bills, health
concerns, and the fog
of eternity. Imagine you pat
your leg, lift the child
onto your lap, wrap
your arms around his thin
frame, and hug him tight,
so tight, as if to absorb him.
Imagine you decide
to say an important thing,
to warn the child
of the vagaries of old
age, but instead, you say
"Enjoy this one-wild-life."
"I'm so happy he says,
then fades into
the comfort of your
cardigan.

Alicia Kimberly

Psalm 23

in my day-clothes, i fall asleep to sirens, grimy like the water
i was baptized in, i have never been clean, not really.
i didn't press the petals of that night in a book; i raked them

with the compost so the memory would tear at the edges,
riddle with moth-hole-mildew, disintegrate if i ever tried
to pick it up, to trace the illustrations with bitten fingernails,

to read the story back to myself.
all i can hear is dry ash leaves wind-skitting the pavement
out the open window. all i feel is the dark.

only the hands linger, blurred dreamlike --i can no longer count
them
but i know there were more thumbs than buttons on my sweater,
heavy-solid and brown like brass, they still flatten me face-down.

i feel somenights that there is no shepherd in this sun-valley.
the slow and the weak are picked off by wolf-lions and shotguns;
the ones who wander in the storm drown themselves in rain.

little girls' cups runneth over while they're held to soot-
stained mattresses, the weight of the cross
swinging hope from the ends of their necklaces.

CONTRIBUTORS

Umar O. Abdul is a Nigerian playwright of Igala origin. He has published *Soyinka Lied, The Making of Tomorrow, The Surrogate, Ashes* (with Kenneth Weene), *The Rightful King* (with Kenneth Weene), *The Broken Moon, Owailo, Frozen Frame, The Inheritor, Stray Bullet and King's Darling.*

Married and blessed with beautiful children, Umar resides in Ankpa, Nigeria where he lectures with the department of Theatre Arts, Kogi State College of Education.

Artiste (Artiste-te) was born in Chicago and now lives and works in Scottsdale, Arizona.

Jimmy Broccoli is a Library Branch Manager by day and a published poet by night with a mission to inspire his readers through imaginative poetic storytelling. He enjoys walks on the beach and playing with puppies.

John Daleiden is retired from 43 years of teaching Language Arts in Iowa Public Schools. Now living in the Phoenix, AZ area, John continues his love of writing, especially writing poetry, and his desire to encourage others to write. His work has appeared in many magazines and anthologies. John has also provided his guidance as an editor and webmaster as well as by moderating groups for the Phoenix Writers' Meetup.

Rosemarie Dombrowski is the inaugural Poet Laureate of Phoenix, AZ, the founding editor of rinky dink press, and the founding director of Revisionary Arts, a nonprofit that facilitates therapeutic poetry workshops for vulnerable populations and the community at large. She's published three collections of poetry and teaches at ASU.

Jack Evans wrote his first poem in 1968. He moved from the banks of the Hudson to the banks of the Agua Fria (Arizona) in 1976. He was a featured artist at the Bisbee Poetry Festival in 1991. He is currently part of the Evans Bell Conversion, a spoken word, music collaborative.

Cynthia Hogue's most recent collections are *Revenance*, listed as one of the 2014 "Standout" books by the Academy of American Poets, and *In June the Labyrinth* (2017). Her tenth collection, *instead, it is dark,* will be out from Red Hen Press in April of 2023. Her third book-length translation (with Sylvain Gallais) is Nicole Brossard's *Distantly* (Omnidawn 2022). Her Covid chapbook is entitled *Contain* (Tram Editions 2022). Among her honors are a Fulbright Fellowship to Iceland, two NEA Fellowships, and the Harold Morton Landon Translation Award from the Academy of American Poets (2013). She served as Guest Editor for Poem-a-Day for September (2022), sponsored by the Academy of American Poets. Hogue was the inaugural Maxine and Jonathan Marshall Chair in Modern and Contemporary Poetry at Arizona State University. She lives in Tucson.

Alicia Kimberly (editor) is a mother of two precocious and funny daughters. Currently living and working in Chandler, Arizona she studied literature and English at Arizona State University, and poetry at Scottsdale Community College. Originally from Indiana and Wisconsin, but now firmly transplanted to Arizona, her poetry is influenced by her experiences, her family, fantasy and mythology, and is unbound by all the "what if's." She has published in *Bonfire of Poetry* so that she is not outdone by her first daughter who has taken up pen and paper.

Michael Mark is the author of *Visiting Her in Queens is More Enlightening than a Month in a Monastery in Tibet* which won the Rattle Chapbook prize in 2022. His poems have recently appeared in Copper Nickel, Grist, The Moth, Pleiades, Ploughshares, Poetry Northwest, The Sun. michaeljmark.com

Adamu Ibrahim Mohammed was born on the 18th day of August, 1982. Attended St. Charles College Ankpa in Kogi state Nigeria. He obtained his HND in Marketing from The Federal Polytechnic Idah also in Kogi state. Currently he is the Vice Principal Administration of Aleka Academy Ankpa. Amongst his poem are: Suicide, Ejeh Road and The Sane Mad Man.

Earnest A. Shoemate is a retired electrical engineer, raised in Oklahoma. He and his wife, Debra, now live in the north central Cross Timbers where he walks the countryside, takes photos, tinkers with gadgets, plants, the minds of others, and whatever else catches his eye; an old man at play.

Carol Tahir is a retired cosmetologist. She lives in a scenic valley in Southern California with her husband of many years. Her works have appeared in other anthologies, online blogs and journals. She loves to read, paint and write.

Susan Vespoli lives in Phoenix, Arizona, where she relies on the power of writing to stay sane. Her poems have been published in *Rattle, Mom Egg Review, Nasty Women Poets: An Unapologetic Anthology of Subversive Verse,* and other cool spots. She is the author of two books, *Blame It on the Serpent* (Finishing Line Press, 2022) and *Cactus as Bad Boy* (Kelsay Books, July 2022).

For five years, **Charles Watts** edited Seizure, a literary journal. His books include "Cure Cottage", "Raptures", "Waking Up in a Beautiful Room", and "The Road to Swat". He lives in Charleston, SC and Lake Placid, NY.

Sometimes **Ken Weene** (editor) writes to exorcise demons. Sometimes he writes because the characters in his head demand to be heard. Sometimes he writes because he thinks what he has to say might amuse or even on occasion inform. Mostly, however, he writes because it is a cheaper addiction than drugs, an easier exercise than going to the gym, and a more sociable outlet than sitting at McDonald's drinking coffee with other old farts: in brief because it keeps him just a bit younger and more alive.

Ken's stories and poetry have appeared in numerous publications and he has a number of published books and plays. Coursing, his collection of poetry, was published in 2022. You can find more at his website www.kennethweene.com

CChristy White (editor) has written poetry since she could first write, and composed haiku-like poems even earlier which her mother wrote down for her. She has self-published several chapbooks of poetry, and her poems have been published in various journals in Arizona, around the country, and in online journals nationally and internationally. Many poems have won awards…modest compensations included! She has hosted several poetry reading series for poets of many backgrounds. She was treasurer for the Tucson Poetry Festival for several years and has been involved with the Arizona State Poetry Society since 1996, holding various nominated and appointed offices including a long term as president which office was recently relinquished to another poet passionate about creating community. In 2017, Christy earned her Master's in Creative Writing/Poetry from Wilkes University. She has given workshops on poetry as a healing modality, and has read at poetry readings across the country and in Scotland. The COVID years have found her on Zoom readings either as participant, host or supporter of poetry. Her day job as an accountant and HR Director has paid for her poetry habit. How could it be any better than that? In the works is a book of memoir poetry. She has also published a monthly Poetry Missive for Arizona poets since July 2012.

Tanya Whitney, retired US Army, began writing poetry a few years ago as part of her PTSD therapy. Her award-winning poetry primarily deals with her military service but has also written other pieces. She has individual poems and short stories published in several anthologies. Author of *A Soldier's Journey Home.*

Mark Young (editor) was born in Leavenworth, KS. He graduated from the University of Kansas with a degree in English and Pacific University with an MFA in Creative Writing. Mark has been married for 41 years and enjoys time with his family, including granddaughter Ramona. For 28 years, Mark served as an American Baptist pastor. Since 2016, he has worked as the President/CEO of Mesa United Way. He continues to write poetry while working as an adjunct professor and a fledgling jazz musician.

Cheryl Renee Long was born in Ventura, California, but has lived in Washington State all her life. A watercolor painter by twelve years old, she now lives, paints and teaches in Ellensburg, Washington. Long is inspired the by wild and remote landscapes and birds of Washington State. She teaches and exhibits her art at Gallery One Visual Arts Center in Ellensburg, WA. She lives with her husband Thomas Long and their golden retriever Juneau and marmalade cat Tenzing. Her art is widely collected and is for sale on her website CherylRLong.com. I also added it as properly formatted below.

www.ingramcontent.com/pod-product-compliance
Lightning Source LLC
Chambersburg PA
CBHW031401160726

47993CB00003B/1071